Eight Preachers Go to Hell

Eight Preachers Go to Hell
Reflections on the place no one wants to go

Open Waters Publishing
700 Prospect Avenue
Cleveland, Ohio 44115
openwaterspublishing.com

Design by Ted Dawson Studio

Printed in the United States of America

10 9 8 7 6 5 4 3 2 1

Open Waters Publishing is an imprint of The Pilgrim Press.
The Open Waters Publishing name and logo are trademarks
of Local Church Ministries, the United Church of Christ.

ISBN 9780-8298-2028-750595

CONTENTS

Introduction

You may think you already know everything about hell that you need to know. As the writers of this book, we thought we did, too. That was before we gave ourselves the assignment to investigate further and find out what we really thought.

This little book doesn't exhaust the subject of hell, but instead opens a few new windows on it. Hell shows up in curses ("Go to hell!"), in therapy sessions, in many of our hymns, and less often in the Bible than most people think. It was not a favorite subject of Jesus. The person sitting next to you in your pew doesn't necessarily think what you think. Hell is big enough to manage multiple perspectives.

Hell is also a metaphor that is rarely examined. Here we dissect it and take a deeper look at its source in ourselves and in our theologies.

Martin Copenhaver argues that heaven and hell are the same place. He drives us to a deeper sense of consequence in our daily living. My own perspective humors you into knowing what you can't know and adds a dimension of mystery to the matter. Mary Luti does the same, only from a much more erudite place. "Damned if I know," she says, joining Martin in driving us, nevertheless, to a sense of consequence about our living, our dying, our heavens and our hells.

Matt Fitzgerald plays with another expression: "Hell, yes!" Doubt about the existence of hell doesn't mean that our behavior is not fraught with the possibilities of both sin and virtue. Matt Laney advises us never to play charades with the concepts of sudden heart attacks or hell. He is aware of how much he doesn't know—and has enough sense to be afraid of human pain and suffering, that which we cause by our actions or inaction, or that which comes to those we love.

Ken Samuel is convinced that hell is the narrow place, the place where there are no good choices, the box we can't get out of. Like prison or an estranged child, hell is the place from which you cannot escape. Quinn Caldwell argues that hell can happen during life as well as after life; meaning that sin is hell. Sin is being curved in on yourself. He sees heaven as the place where you can be more flexible, and stand up straight. Lillian Daniel finds hell on a highway stop, and then stops to consider heaven instead.

Notably, many of us see a hyper self-consciousness as hellish. Two words keep coming up. One is "mirror." When all we can see is in the mirror, we are in hell. The other word that comes up often is "Hitler." No one assigned Hitler to either heaven or hell, with most of the writers opting for a more universal salvation. But he sure did bother everyone.

When we finished the writing of this book, there was a sense that we had all gotten close to the fire and brimstone, but had not been burned. We sensed a stronger desire to make good choices and to create environments where more people had more access to good choices. We found ourselves tinged with the possibility of sin as well as salvation, a way to look up as well as to look down.

Donna Schaper

Heaven and Hell
Are the Same Place

Martin B. Copenhaver

▼　▼　▼

The traditional images of what happens when we die are that we face an eternal fork in the road with two divergent ways that lead to two very different places. One road ascends to a place of light, bliss and communion with God. That place is called heaven. The other road descends to a place of darkness and torment, a place of fire, where God is absent. That place is called hell. When we die, God (the perfect judge) determines which road we must take and whether heaven or hell will be our home for all eternity.

These images can be so firmly planted in our minds that we might be surprised to see how tenuously they are rooted in the words of scripture. Traditional pictures of heaven and hell owe more to works of literature, such as Dante's *Divine Comedy* and John Milton's *Paradise Lost*, than they do to scripture.

I believe heaven and hell are the same place. Or, to be more precise, heaven and hell are the same place, but two very different experiences. That is, when we die, we all enter into the eternal presence of God. Some will experience that as heaven and others as hell.

If we have spent our lives serving and praising God, when we die into the eternal presence of God, it will be the fulfillment of our desire. What we have longed for all our lives, communion with God, will be ours, and we will know the bliss we associate with heaven.

But if, instead, we have spent our lives disobeying and denying God, when we die into the eternal presence of God, it will be a very different experience. To face the God whom we have disobeyed and denied, and to face in God's presence the truth about our lives, is to know some of the torment and remorse we associate with hell.

In this sense, when we die we will all experience divine judgment. In the pure and unambiguous presence of God, there will remain not a single illusion to which we can cling. A friend once told me that her understanding of divine judgment would be to have friends, family, and God all in a screening room showing a film of her life—her actions, her words, her thoughts—and those present asking, "Barbara, you did this?" and, "Barbara, you said that?" It is a sobering image, but I think it is an apt one.

To have a clear and searching light on our actions, to see them in all of their clarity and consequences for the first time in the pure and purifying presence of God is itself a form of punishment. Dante said in his epic poem, *The Inferno*, that in hell the punishment is "the sin itself, experienced without illusion." If we think that this softens the concept of divine judgment, or if we are comforted by it, then perhaps it is because we have yet to imagine fully what it would be like to finally see ourselves without illusion.

If after our deaths we must survey our lives from God's point of view—that is, without illusion—then we are also invited to see from God's point of view that we can be made new. We do not know how God will eventually draw us all into full communion—God has many ways to woo us. Certainly, some of those ways are not limited to our earthly lives.

Peanut farmer and Greek scholar, Clarence Jordan, used to say: "Imagine that a man has led a sinful life and has never given much thought to God. Now he is walking along, taking stock of his life, and he says to himself, 'Perhaps I should change my ways and turn my life over to God. Yes, I think I'm ready to do that.' And as he continues like this, he crosses a train track. At that very moment, a freight train comes barreling down the track and kills him. Jordan then asked if we could imagine God saying, 'Blast it! If only that freight train hadn't come along just at that moment, I could have got him!'" That is, even though our experience is bounded by birth on one end and death on the other, we should not assume the right to limit God's work to the same arena.

When I once said something like this in a sermon, someone who had served in World War II was incensed: "Do you mean I will have to share eternity with Hitler? I want no part of that!" He thought I was saying that the Hitler with whom he would share eternity would be the same murderous Hitler he had known in this life. But after experiencing the purifying, redeeming presence of God, even the most degenerate of us can be transformed. So, yes, after death we may share communion with Hitler, but this Hitler will not be the tyrant of history. He will be the transformed Hitler of divine eternity, redeemed by the love of a God whose searching love is not limited by the span of our earthly life and who will not rest until we are all found.

Dante, Siri and the Ultimate Bad Selfie

Matt Laney

▼   ▼   ▼

It's been said the worst time to have a heart attack is during a game of charades. Likewise the worst time to entertain thoughts about hell is when you are having a heart attack. It doesn't help. So please, if you are experiencing any signs of physical distress, stop reading now.

We'll start off on safe, familiar ground. While we have a few everyday expressions about heaven (Well for heaven's sake!) we are positively hell-bent when it comes to working that four letter word into our patterns of speech. Here's a random sample:

The road to hell is paved with good intentions.
Well that's gone to hell in a handbasket!
I feel like I've been to hell and back!
Let's get the hell out of here.

There will be hell to pay.

The hell you are!

Hell on wheels.

Give 'em hell!

Hell yeah!

Hell no.

What the hell are we talking about?

Suppose, for example, someone tells you to "Go to hell!" You might be offended or even confused because the directive is never followed by directions. It is assumed you already know how to get there as if you are the bad guy in a formula action movie who's getting his just desserts at the hands of the righteous hero in the final scene. In that case, as you take your final breath, your eyes will widen with terror at the prospect of suffering eternal punishment for all the misery you've caused in the last two hours of the film.

But let's just say you are not the villain in a B movie but an altogether decent and respectable "real" person who feels that her chances of ending up in hell are about as good as being drafted for the NBA. Like the vast majority of most people in some places you are undoubtedly, unquestionably skeptical about the existence of a literal hell and therefore you have a snowball's chance in hell of actually showing up there. Even so, you still have a good picture in your mind of what hell is. We all do. Hell is that eternally burning horror-house staffed by pointy-eared, pitchfork-wielding demons who love to torture already tormented souls much like children who love to fry bugs with a magnifying glass.

Where does that image come from and why do we keep gravitating to it? Well, consider how many times you've walked into the kitchen and can't remember why, but for some reason you think you'll find a clue in the refrigerator. The vision of hell in the not-very-funny *Divine Comedy* written by Dante in 1320 A.D. is like that fridge . . . in more ways than one.

According to Dante, hell has demons, torment and fires aplenty but the deepest place of hell is frozen rather than fiery which makes sense for a guy from Italy where the average temperature is a balmy 70 degrees. Apocryphal history has it (so apocryphal you won't find it anywhere but here) that Dante once traveled to Antarctica where he proclaimed "It's colder than hell down here!" right before high tailing it back to Florence to enshrine that insight at the end of his epic poem which is now required reading for most high school students, especially the chapters on lust and gluttony, right before prom weekend.

Don't get me wrong. Hell might be exactly like Dante's long, strange, drain-circling slide from a topless tropical beach to a frozen prison of ice. That pretty well fits my image of hell. It is an icy-cold, frozen tundra where we are utterly alone; a place where misery does not love company, because hell is a realm of pure isolation; the logical extension of a soul that has totally failed to discover the point of life. What's the point of life?

Pick up an iPhone and ask Siri "What is the meaning of life?" and you will get answers ranging from "42," a reference to *The Hitchhiker's Guide to the Galaxy*, a Divine Comedy of another sort, to "I Kant answer that. Ha Ha!" to "All evidence to date suggests it's chocolate" to "I don't know but I think there's an app for that."

If you ask a true Calvinist, he or she would quote the Westminster Catechism and tell you the meaning of life is "to glorify God and to enjoy Him forever."

With all due respect to artificial intelligence fabricated by people who would like nothing more than to claim every penny you have, I'm going with the Westminster Catechism on this one. If the purpose of my life is to glorify God and rejoice in God forever then the converse is also true: glorifying myself, seeking my own way, putting myself on God's throne is a blatant exercise in missing the point.

So if I were asked to re-write the Divine Comedy, I would have hell paved with mirrors. Big gaudy mirrors with overstated gold frames. Heck, the whole of hell might be a house of mirrors! In the middle of the house is a throne, a miniature version of God's throne, where the self-accursed soul sits for all time admiring its reflection from every possible angle.

While it is inappropriate to imagine God roasting the damned like marshmallows over an eternal fire, I'm not ruling out the possibility of a hellish afterlife characterized by isolation, sorrow and self-worship. Is it possible that these souls could be liberated from their prison of miserable self-obsession? I'm not ruling that out either. It all depends on whether we are willing to surrender the throne, in this life or in the next, to its proper occupant . . . for heaven's sake. What could be more glorious than letting God be God and what could be more *terrifying* than thinking we are up for the job?

Damned if I Know

Mary Luti

▼   ▼   ▼

When I was a child, I believed life had three possible destinations—Hell, a place for the irredeemably wicked; Purgatory, a way-station for souls who need tidying up before entering Heaven; and Heaven, where the good live forever with God.

Hell was a lurid place full of torment, bright red demons, and the awful shrieks of the damned. It was awful, but nothing about it seemed unjust to me. The wicked had had their chances and blown them. They'd exercised free will, messed up, and thereby *chosen* Hell. God was not a villain for damning them; God respected their decision.

I knew I'd go to Hell if I messed up too—committed "mortal sin" or broke the laws of the Church. It didn't take much back then. You didn't have to be an axe-murderer. Just miss Mass on Sunday with no good excuse, then get hit by a truck before you could go to confession, and down you went. We looked both ways a lot back then.

I didn't want to go to Hell, of course, but my overriding memory of pondering Hell wasn't anxiety. It was sadness. It staggered me that Hell had no exit. Sleepless in bed, I'd repeat, "Forever and ever and ever and ever and ever and ever…" trying to measure Hell's horrific eternity. It left me feeling unutterably bereft. No one in Hell would ever, *ever* see God. As contradictory as it seems for one so blithely accepting of the awful justice of God, I'd always found God inexpressibly desirable. Not to be with God was the worst thing I could imagine.

The spiritual cosmology of my childhood is long gone— no more gauzy Heaven up there, sulfuric Hell down there, and blah Purgatory in between. But the thought of Hell still makes me indescribably sad. I am still left desolate by the thought that there could be, even theoretically, a place devoid of God.

I don't want Hell to exist. I don't think God does, either. But it's easy for me to say that. One can say anything one wants about something no one knows a thing about, really. Still, when the question of eternal salvation is posed in traditional terms, my first impulse is to rule no one out, even though such un-picky inclusion carries a moral risk. It can appear not to take evil, sin, or justice seriously.

But universalism is a far less violent option than its

opposite, so I want it to be true. And why not? Ruling people in or out is not an innocuous theological exercise. It isn't theoretical. It has consequences. If somebody thinks you're unworthy of God in the next life, they probably think you're unworthy of God in this life, too. Thus history is littered with the battered bodies of everybody's excluded infidels, sinners, and heretics.

All the same, while I believe that God wills the healing and restoration of all creatures on the New Earth to which Heaven comes down, I don't know if God's purpose is accomplished in every case. Call it pessimism, or a bracing awareness of my own secret perversity, but I also believe human beings are capable of willing their own destruction, individually and socially. What this means in practice, I don't know. I can't imagine. Just thinking about it causes me revulsion. Yet we ignore at our own peril the human capacity to thwart God's intentions.

Jesus regarded it with utmost seriousness. Some of his hardest sayings concern what's in store for us who stubbornly resist God's healing will by our determination to seek at the expense of others the gratification of own desires. The way we conduct our lives has consequences beyond our bodily boundaries, vast consequences for which we are in fact responsible.

The tenacity with which the Church has held the doctrine of Hell right into this post-modern age testifies to a deep conviction—namely, that everything in the outcome of a human life is at stake in the way we use our God-given freedom. This conviction can't lightly be set aside. Sometimes I think human freedom is more fearsome than Hell.

Of course, freedom and responsibility are notoriously hard to nail down. Much of the time, sin is more a matter of haplessness than will. Our choices are never simple, fully free, or obvious. Our motives are never uncomplicated or even fully conscious. We are so thirsty for love that we're prepared to do almost anything to satisfy our need. These things should and do mitigate our responsibility. But who is to say with assuring clarity how to weigh them? And who knows whether in the end they absolve us so completely that something like Hell becomes unnecessary?

Weighing them and absolving us, we believe with relief, is the task of Christ, who embodies the God in whom justice and mercy are not incompatible. The gospels also insist, and scandalize us when they do, that in God's economy we "deserve" undeserved mercy, when in our economy the judgment would surely be otherwise.

This is the only educated guess, and the only comfort that allows me to live (sort of) unafraid. This is the comfort that allows me to live, period. It's all I've got. It's all I want.

As for Hell, damned if I know.

Hell, Yes?

Matt Fitzgerald

▼　▼　▼

Fifteen years ago I stood in my first pulpit and proclaimed that hell does not exist. My congregation did not seem particularly relieved. Ten years ago I used etymological arguments and word studies to put the devil's fires out. People looked bored. I grew a bit more shrill. Five years ago I proclaimed that the grace of God is so good it will overwhelm whatever punishment we might deserve, rendering hell empty even if it *did* exist.

Crickets.

Last year I practically pounded the pulpit as I announced that the ultimate expression of God's power was to give away control, to die and then to rise from a disgraced grave in order to pull *everyone* among us up to heaven in his wake. No one raised an eyebrow.

I've been preaching against damnation for fifteen years. I've proclaimed the non-existence of hell to four different churches and thousands of Christians and I've been met with yawning indifference every time.

Why? Well, on the one hand, liberal Protestantism has done so thorough a job of declaring the goodness of God that we have forgotten about God's judgment. And on the other hand liberal Protestantism has done such a good job of declaring the loveliness of humanity that we don't think we're deserving of God's judgment anyhow.

Either way, the threat of hell does not seem real. Couple our theological optimism with the cartoonish depictions of hellfire popular culture has planted in our imaginations and damnation becomes quite easy to dismiss.

So, it appears that I am standing in the pulpit full to bursting with this kind of gospel: "Guess what? Dragons don't exist! And werewolves are a myth!" I'm preaching the non-existence of hell to a tradition that stopped believing in it decades ago. It isn't good news. It is yesterday's news.

And it may be wrong. If all I do is stand in the pulpit and tell people what they already believe about God I collude against the Holy Spirit. How can God blow through the church and turn things upside down if we've closed the windows?

The church is at its worst when preachers proudly reinforce their congregations' existing biases. God doesn't work in an echo chamber. We ought to talk to ourselves of course, but we shouldn't mistake our own ideas for divine truth.

Divine truth comes "from above, not below" as Karl Barth reminds us. This means that our convictions may be just that—*our* convictions. Today's liberal Protestant disbelief in hell may simply be the product of our age and its inclinations, just as a prior era's crippling salvation anxiety grew out of its age and attending uneasiness.

Meanwhile, the word of God stands above the sands of time and insists that God is more complex than the unavoidable mercy I've spent more than a decade explaining.

A few weeks ago my six-year-old son wandered into my office and picked up a child's Bible. The Ten Commandments were inscribed on the inside cover. He read the first few out loud in a disinterested voice, but then got intrigued by the command to "Honor the Sabbath day." I explained what it meant and he said, "But you work on Sunday." I replied by paraphrasing an old Barth quote, "Praising God isn't work," and he responded, "Well, you sure get up early."

He kept on reading. He stumbled over some words, but the message leapt cleanly into the room. I fell silent. As he reminded me to honor my parents, to refrain from lying, stealing, coveting I found it far more difficult to explain my transgressions away. God's law hung in the air and I felt judged. I was judged. I am judged.

Over and over again scripture insists that God will judge us. As Revelation has it: "Then I saw a great white throne and the one who sat on it; the earth and the heaven fled from his presence, and no place was found for them. And I saw the dead, great and small, standing before the throne, and books were opened. Also another book was opened, the book of life. And the dead were judged according to their works, as recorded in the books. And the sea gave up the dead that were in it, Death and Hades gave up the dead that were in them, and all were judged according to what they had done. Then Death and Hades were thrown into the lake of fire. This is the second death, the lake of fire; and anyone whose name was not found written in the book of life was thrown into the lake of fire."

I read those words and I immediately try to dismiss them. They're from the *Book of Revelation after all*. Isn't it just an extended allegory? Isn't God a giant softie? Isn't my preaching a weekly echo chamber, saying nothing new, but nothing ancient either, just a sweet celebration of what my people and I want to hear?

My son's voice rings in my ears. I remember what God asks of me, I consider how I'm living my life and I swear, my heart rate increases. So I do what Luther said we ought to do in such circumstances. I go running toward Jesus. Here is how he answers my request to please erase God's expectations: "Love your neighbor as yourself."

It doesn't help. I am writing this on a Monday morning. I live in a city where eight people were shot and killed over the weekend, while I grilled dinner and drank wine. I don't love my neighbors. I ignore them. What if the lake of fire is a gesture toward something real? What if God's judgment burns like fire?

Generations ago ministers felt guilt about keeping their doubt out of the pulpit. 19th century Congregationalist preachers agonized about whether or not to confess their increasing skepticism. I am beginning to feel the same way about my creeping suspicion that God's judgment might be real. What will happen if I go public with my doubt in liberal Protestantism's disbelief in hell? Will my parishioners feel as anxious as I do? Maybe their knees will knock and they will tremble before the prospect of God's all-consuming holiness. Maybe we'll all have no choice but to drop to our knees and beg Christ for the mercy we surely don't deserve. And maybe, at that moment, we'll discover who God truly is.

The Highway to Hell

Lillian Daniel

▼　▼　▼

We had split our Connecticut household into two vehicles loaded up for a cross-country drive into a new life in Illinois. I left first, with my eleven year-old son, a ten-year-old dog, and essential items like my favorite pillow from a childhood spent in seven countries.

At my first sighting of corn, I was amazed. I had never seen corn in person before. Up until that moment, golden fields were the stuff of fantasy, like baseball movies and truck commercials.

At first it was beautiful. It looked as though it had been there forever, steady, strong and straight.

What kind of person hasn't seen corn before? When I got to Chicago, was there going to be a quiz? If there was this huge gap in my experience of maize and other agricultural matters, what else was I missing?

I felt rootless.

I recalled that ever since accepting the call, people had asked me the same question again and again. "So do you have family out here?"

"Chicago's a big city," I would respond. "I thought anybody could move here."

But driving rootless through the corn, I wondered if I was moving to a place populated only by people who already had people who lived there.

"You don't have any family in the Midwest at all? Then what's bringing you here?"

I began to perseverate on the frightening plot line of a horror movie I had seen as a youth, *Children of the Corn*. In that film, a cult full of evil Midwestern blonde children offer human sacrifices to a bloodthirsty corn god, preying mostly on over–confident road trippers from out East.

At what seemed to be a midway point in Indiana, I pulled up at the hotel I had carefully booked in advance, to make sure it was suitable for our ten-year old dog. It was a decrepit establishment that boasted live strippers "Rated XXX" amidst the cornfields. A confederate flag in neon lights lit up with the hotel's restaurant. A more modest handwritten sign announced, "Your dog is welcome."

I pulled back onto the highway to look for a better place to stay, only to see a giant billboard that declared in enormous letters, "HELL IS REAL!"

No kidding, I thought to myself. Hell was real and I was in it.

It's now been more than a decade since I became a sojourner in a strange land called the Midwest. I've seen that wacky sign too many times to count. It doesn't bother me anymore. I no longer suspect that wacky bloodthirsty children are hiding in the corn. In fact, I have since learned that many people around here came from somewhere else, just like I did. And we call this place home.

So when I think of Hell in eternal terms, I no longer think it's a sketchy motel, a cultish corn community or even a long, boring, flat highway.

But I do think that hell is a place where you do not feel at home. Hell is a place on the other side of this life where you still wonder if you belong. In hell, you are a stranger in a strange land who has made hotel reservations that will not come through as planned.

I contrast this to the idea of heaven. The Bible talks about a heavenly banquet, where everyone will be fed. I imagine heaven as a giant dinner party; with everyone I have ever loved and everyone who has ever loved me will be gathered together, with Jesus, God and the Holy Spirit.

And I will be seated next to all three of them. I know it's physically impossible to sit next to three people, but in heaven, those physical limitations won't matter. Either that, or I'll be sitting on one of their laps.

This last part is, of course, my self-centered fantasy of heaven. Just like that highway in Indiana was my self-centered fantasy of hell. Both were all about me: my fears, my insecurities and my judgment.

In the real heavenly banquet, I suspect the guest list will probably be way longer than any list I would come up with. And I suspect the seating arrangements will be different too. I base this upon my belief that Jesus will be running things in a manner consistent with how he lived on earth.

Given that, I suspect I will also see all the people who have ever irritated me. I'll see all the people who have hurt me and all the people who have let me down. Even worse, I suspect the guest list will include all the people that I have disappointed, betrayed and injured. And they may well be the ones sitting next to Jesus, while I am stuck at the end of the line asking some bureaucratic angel to look again for my nametag.

This heavenly banquet is sounding less and less appealing to me. What if a bothersome kid from third grade sits between me and the grandfather I never met on earth? What if my quality time with Jesus gets taken over by that compulsive talker from my last job? What if the whole banquet is so disappointing that I decide to leave heaven, and check out my other options? Why wouldn't I take my chances and get back on the road?

Having left heaven over its lack of admissions standards, I'd be on the highway to hell. A big road sign might announce once again "HELL IS REAL!" but this time it would have more meaning. Unlike in life, where we write those signs to warn other people, this one might seem like it was for me. Hell is real, and I chose that path.

That road is the never-ending suspicion that there could be something better out there than living life with all the broken people God loves anyway.

So for now, my challenge in this limited, earthly, three-dimensional life is to avoid that never-ending highway of discontent and prepare instead for the banquet. Both will be open to me. But based on what I've practiced in this life, which one will I be open to?

No Other Way in Hell

Kenneth L. Samuel

▼ ▼ ▼

A man died and went straight to hell. Upon his arrival, he looked around and thought to himself, "This isn't so bad." In the first place, hell had air conditioning. And he noticed that a lot of his friends were there. There was a copious spread of food on a nearby table, wonderful mood lighting and nice music emanating from a thumping sound system as people mingled and chatted.

A very attractive woman approached the man and asked: "Would you like to dance?" He responded: "Sure!" So they stepped out on the dance floor, and he had a great time as he showed off his best dance moves while she smiled and giggled.

But after dancing and laughing for a while, he grew tired, so he said to the woman: "Thanks for the dance. I think I'll stop now and go get refreshed."

She looked at him squarely and replied: "No, you can't do that. You have forgotten that this is hell. And in hell, everyone must keep dancing to the same music with the same partner. And the music never stops."

This story was told by Howard Thurman. It is his depiction of hell. It is also mine. Hell, for me, is any place or any situation in which there are no options.

Growing up poor in the South Bronx of New York City did not present very many options for me. Life in the ghetto rarely does. There are cycles of co-dependency, cycles of addiction and cycles of dysfunction that are reinforced and perpetuated by cycles of poverty. And there are many who meander within the ghetto confines of few to no options all of their lives.

But thank God for the options to ghetto life that were presented to me through the church and through education. The church said to me: "You can choose a life that is more abundant. You can choose a life that is governed by a faith in God who makes all things possible. You do not have to be limited by your circumstances, because through Christ, all things are possible.

Education said to me: "There is a world beyond the conditions of your current circumstances. Knowledge and intelligence can take you there. If you apply yourself to your educational pursuit, you will have options in your career and options in your lifestyle that will open the world to you."

I made a choice to take advantage of both those options.

Neither of them has disappointed. The avoidance of hell for me has been in the availability of options.

But for those who perceive that they have no options, life is a living hell. No option to low wages. No option to substandard education. No option to low income housing. No option to poverty, dysfunction and co-dependency. No options for the future.

No options can easily give way to feelings of desperation. And desperation can easily give way to mindsets of despair. And people who live with despair pose a grave danger to themselves and to others.

This is the hell that threatens all of us—whether it comes from the person in the simmering ghettos of America or the person in the volatile regions of the Middle East.

The answer to desperation and despair is in providing accessible, affordable, viable options for better living. With viable options, the onus is on the individual. Without viable options, the onus is upon all of us. And we all will surely catch hell if we do not work to ensure that viable options are available to everyone.

We cannot exist peacefully as an island of plenty and abundant options in a sea of poverty and few to no options.

The prospect of spending eternity in hell—a place of no options, is precisely what motivates me to take full advantage of every option that is currently made available to me by God's Amazing Grace. To have choices in life is a privilege. And each of our decisions does have consequences.

In Deuteronomy 30:19, God says to God's people: "I have set before you life and death, blessing and cursing: therefore choose life, that both thou and thy seed may live."

The choice to live is divinely endowed to everyone and should be reflected in everyone's inalienable right to life, liberty and the pursuit of happiness.

But if we choose despair instead of hope; if we choose defeat instead of perseverance; if we limit our temporal lives by choosing not to be open to eternal possibilities, we, in essence, choose to go to hell. Our choices have generational and eternal consequences.

Life is a choice. Hell is either reneging on that choice, or having no choice at all.

Straight Out of Hell

Quinn G. Caldwell

▼　▼　▼

Some say that sin is nothing more than a turning inward upon oneself. It's choosing to focus on your own worries, your own needs, your own accomplishments, your own loves or hungers, the wrongs the world has done you and the things you think you're owed that the world has not yet given to you. It's curling yourself and your life all up into a ball so that all you can see is yourself and all you can hear is your own muttering.

Some say the Christian life, on the other hand, the life of virtue, is like a great flowering, an endless opening out into the world. It's learning to see the people around you, to hear them, to notice their cries and their needs. It's turning outward toward the world until your back is straight and your eyes are clear and you move through the world leading with your heart.

Some say Heaven is like a city paved with gold and walled with jewels and gated with pearls that stand open all day long. And there's a party up in there, and the people live right in the heart of God. Some watch from the ramparts for newcomers, and when they see you arrive there outside the city, they blow the trumpets. They clap and wave and cheer to welcome you home.

And some say this: when one day you show up outside that city, you will show up in the posture you've spent your life cultivating.

If you've spent your life on virtue, then you will show up straight-backed and clear-eyed and sharp-eared. You will hear the trumpet sound, you will see the city shining there before you like the sun, and you will hear them shout for joy as you sprint home through those gates.

But if you've spent your life on sin, then you will show up outside that city all curled up into a ball. You will not see the jeweled walls or the pearly gates, because you will be staring at your own crotch. You will not hear the trumpets and the cheering, because you will be listening to yourself muttering your favorite litany, the song of your own accomplishments or the bitter dirge of all the ways the world hasn't given you what you think you want. You will not want to move, because your arms and legs will have twisted themselves around your torso to keep you protected from the world. And if you would only look up, or shut up, or loosen up, you would see the glory there in front of you and realize there's nothing but you keeping you from going in. But there you will spend eternity, they say, all twisted up in a ball just feet from heaven, and not even know it's there. And that, they say, will be hell.

All that works for me—except for just one word: "eternity." That word is a problem for me because I believe there will be Christians in heaven. Christians won't be the only ones there, I'm sure, but at least some of the people in that city will be followers of Jesus. And if they've spent their whole lives following Jesus, I don't know why they would stop just because they've made it to heaven. If they've spent their lives following the one who feeds the hungry masses, heals the broken, drives out the demons of the haunted, demands justice for the world, blesses sinners and eats with tax collectors, why would they stop in heaven? If they've spent their lives noticing the ones that they believe Jesus would especially love, the ones most in need of care, and heading straight for those ones first, I can't imagine why just being in God's presence all day would break the habit.

So if somebody shows up outside the walls all twisted up in his own little ball of hell, I don't think they're going to just stand there blowing brass at him and wringing their hands because he won't look up. I think they're going to come down off the walls and go get him.

I think they'll do what they've been doing for the world all along:

They will go to him, try to get his attention, say, "Hey, look! God is *right there waiting*."

They'll splash water in her face. They'll do it three times, and you know whose name they'll do it in.

They'll tempt him with good food, bread that smells like heaven and a cup of rich, full-bodied red.

And if none of that works, they'll get right down there in the dust next to her, put their arms around her, and start to sing. They'll lay their hands on that bent head, massage those shoulders until they relax enough to get a hand under the chin, and then they will lift her head until her eyes are looking outward again, and they will point, and they will whisper, "*Look.*"

I know what it feels like to sleep in a funny position all night and then stand up in the morning, so I do not imagine the un-balling will be easy. I do not think the stretch back into a human shape will be painless. In fact, I think it will be very difficult. In fact, I think it will probably be excruciating. Maybe it will feel like someone's poking you all over with pitchforks. Maybe it will feel like burning.

I do not know how long this will take, except that it will not take forever. I assume it will take longer for some of us than for others. I assume that the more time we spend training now, the more lithe we will be when the time comes, that any time we spend in life heads up, shoulders back and leading with our hearts will make it that much easier to straighten up out of hell and walk through the gates of heaven when the time comes.

In fact, I'm counting on it.

One of the Better Curses

Donna Schaper

▼   ▼   ▼

"Go to hell" is one of the better curses. You say it on the
way out after a fight. You mean a big goodbye, not a little one.
Once you have told someone to go to hell, it's pretty hard to
get reacquainted. First of all, they never know when you're
going to say it again. Plus you have given them eternal, not
temporary, advice. Hell is a good curse word because it has a
certain finality to it.

It is also a good curse because you can blame your use of it
on theological misunderstanding. After all, no one knows
where hell is. Or if hell is. Or whether you can get frequent
flyer points on your way there. Or if it is cold like the
cosmopolitan nothingness of superior existentialists or hot like
the great fire of the brimstone bunch. Nor does anyone know
if you are conscious of being in hell or whether your

consciousness—so heavenly—is lost on the way down. Why send someone somewhere, even in a curse, if they won't know that they are there? What if they don't really suffer in hell when what you wanted is for them to suffer? Without consciousness, you can't really enter the Olympics of suffering because you can't find an audience for it. Is there Facebook in hell? How do we alert our friends "back home" about our whereabouts? Do they care? And do we care, once we are in hell, whether they know or not?

If someone gets upset that you cursed them with one of the better curses, you can just say you didn't know what you were saying, which of course is true. Even though we can't know, we have to wonder, along with some of the greatest literature and cartoons of all time. Red-tailed devils, pitchforks, and *Crime and Punishment* all come to mind.

I wonder who else is there? Hitler? My ex-husband? His lover? Nixon? Atheists only or agnostics also? What about those of us without a big sin resumé who neglected to do what we could have done or give a damn about what we could have given a damn about? By the way, "damn you" is also a good curse. It has the same virtues as go to hell.

I also wonder about hell's location. Is it a one-way ticket or can you go round trip? How is the food in hell? The pillows? That is a silly question, of course, because there are no pillows in hell. I can almost guarantee that. Oxymoronic, to put it mildly.

Curses, like anything else, have their strengths and

weaknesses. When it comes to hell, I like to know that I don't know. Of course, what we don't know can kill us. Not knowing about hell doesn't absolve one from heading toward heaven or understanding that life is consequential and that what goes around does come around.

I also like to organize my life towards the very few things I can know. Go to Heaven! There you will face similar questions, but at least you will have exited with blessing and not curse.

Quinn G. Caldwell is the author of *All I Really Want: Readings for a Modern Christmas*. He lives on a small homestead in Upstate New York with his partner, their toddler, and an alarming number of animals. He is the Pastor of Plymouth Congregational Church in Syracuse, New York.

Martin B. Copenhaver is the President of Andover Newton Theological School, Newton Centre, Massachusetts. He is the author of six books, most recently *Jesus is the Question: The 307 Questions Jesus Asked and the 3 He Answered*. Martin also writes for a number of periodicals, including *The Christian Century*, where he serves as an Editor at Large. Martin's other claim to fame is that he once made a television commercial with Larry Bird.

Lillian Daniel is the author of the best-selling *When "Spiritual But Not Religious" is Not Enough: Seeing God in Surprising Places, Even the Church*. Senior Minister of the First Congregational Church of Glen Ellyn, Illinois, her speaking engagements have taken her from Queens College, Ontario to Kings College, London.

Matt Fitzgerald is the Senior Pastor of St. Pauls United Church of Christ in Chicago where he lives in the Lincoln Park neighborhood with his wife and their three young children. He is a frequent contributor to *The Christian Century* magazine. In his younger years he worked at nearly every job a restaurant has to offer, from washing dishes to tending bar.

Matthew Laney is the Senior Minister of Asylum Hill Congregational Church in Hartford, Connecticut. A native New Englander, he has served congregations in Vermont and Michigan and worked with people who are homeless in Atlanta. Matt is a husband, a father and an aspiring novelist for young readers.

Mary Luti is the Interim Senior Pastor of Wellesley Village Church, in Wellesley, Massachusetts. A long time seminary educator and historian, she is the author of *Teresa of Avila's Way* and numerous articles on the practice of the Christian life. She is also the former pastor of First Church in Cambridge (MA), the only woman senior minister in over 375 years of continuing congregational life. She is a founding member of The Daughters of Abraham, a national network of interfaith women's book groups.

Kenneth L. Samuel is the Pastor of Victory for the World Church in Stone Mountain, Georgia, and the author of *Solomon's Success: Four Essential Keys to Leadership*. He is Co-Chair of the African American Leadership Council of People for the American Way, Washington, D.C. and the proud parent of one daughter, Kendalle Marye.

Donna Schaper is the author of 32 books, most recently *Grace at Table: Small Spiritual Solutions to Large Material Problems*, and Senior Minister at Judson Memorial Church in New York City. She grows a superb tomato and has three children, two grandchildren and a husband whom she has known and loved for 32 years. A board member of the New York Civil Liberties Union, Schaper is an enthusiastic activist.